JUNIOR HERITAGE BOOKS

HOUSES

Written and Illustrated by
EDWARD OSMOND

London: B. T. BATSFORD LTD.

ACKNOWLEDGMENT

The Author and Publishers express their thanks to the following photographers whose work is reproduced in this book:—
Aerofilms Ltd. for pp. 46-47; the Trustees of the British Museum for p. 18; the late Brian C. Clayton for pp. 26 and 77 (b); Mr. J. Dixon-Scott for p. 77 (a); Eagle Photos Ltd., Cheltenham, for pp. 70-71; Mr. Herbert Felton for p. 36; Leonard and Marjorie Gayton for p. 2; Mr. A. F. Kersting for pp. 58-59, 62, 66, 75 and 77 (c); Mr. T. H. Mason for p. 77 (d); Mr. Walter Scott for p. 50; Messrs. F. J. Ward for p. 67; Mr. Reece Winstone for pp. 49 and 63; Miss M. E. Wood for p. 31.

First Published, Spring 1956

Printed and bound in Holland by L. Van Leer & Co. Ltd., Amsterdam, for the publishers, B. T. BATSFORD LTD., 4, Fitzhardinge Street, Portman Square, London, W.1.

W.K.Ritchie

8th October 1960

JUNIOR HERITAGE BOOKS

HOUSES

The Illustration on page 2 is of a sixteenth-century street, Elm Hill, Norwich

CONTENTS

OLD STONE AGE

MIDDLE STONE AGE

NEW STONE AGE

BRONZE AGE

IRON AGE
ANNO DOMINI

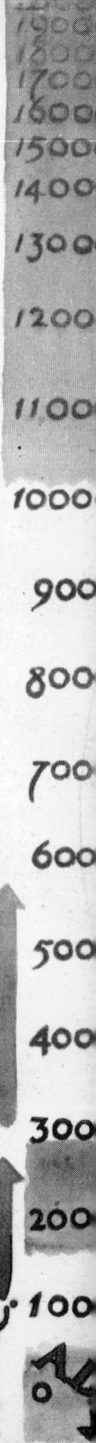

2000
1900
1800
1700
1600
1500
1400
1300
1200
1100
1000
900
800
700
600
500
400
300
200
100
B.C.
A.D.
0

INTRODUCTORY

THE story of houses, unlike that of castles or abbeys, has no clear-cut beginning in historic times. Its early chapters are lost from view in that vast period of time that we call prehistory.

The first hint we have of artificial dwellings in Western Europe belongs to the time when the last of the great Ice Ages was drawing to a close 10,000 years ago or more. At that time the men of the Old Stone Age were hunting reindeer, buffalo and mammoth where the English Channel now lies and across the South of England. During the long bitter winters of those distant days the people lived in natural caves, where they left us paintings of the animals they hoped to kill. These paintings include representations of what appear to be huts; and we believe that during the short summer season they moved out onto the open tundra where they constructed homes, probably of a very temporary nature.

The earliest dwellings of which actual remains have been found in Britain belong to the next long period—the Middle Stone Age. During this time the climate was very gradually becoming milder. The ice-cap in the north was shrinking, and the last glaciers of the ice age were melting away. At the same time the bare tundra was slowly giving place to forest, first of hardy fir and birch, and later, much later, of oak and alder.

As the forests returned the reindeer went away, and the huge mammoths became extinct. The Old Stone Age men departed also, and their place was taken by others who hunted red-deer, beavers and water-fowl in the forest-covered land. These people of the Middle Stone Age scraped out shallow pits in light gravelly soil, and into the circle of earth thrown up around the pits they pushed the branches of trees to form an untidy canopy, possibly adding the bark of trees or the skins of animals to complete the shelter (p. 9).

Primitive peoples may be placed in three groups—hunters, herdsmen and husbandmen (cultivators of land). The most primitive, the hunters, usually move from place to place in search of game; and the herdsmen, too, are often more or less nomadic, moving where the pasture is good. Both these ways of living favour a temporary or portable form of habitation—often merely tents. But the cultivators of the land have to remain where their seed is sewn and in consequence tend to produce sturdy, permanent houses.

It was probably about 2,000 B.C. that this land saw its first farmers. They came by water, for Britain was by that time an island, bringing with them their cattle, sheep and pigs and also the seeds of wheat and rye to sew in small plots near their villages. There were the men of the New Stone Age; and although their primitive methods of cultivation soon exhausted the ground and made it necessary to clear new fields every few years, their existence was settled enough to produce homes of a more substantial kind.

On page 9 we give a drawing of a typical New Stone Age hut. It shows a roughly circular " pit dwelling " hollowed out of the ground like those of earlier times. But now the conical turf roof is supported by sturdy poles whose inner ends are held up by a single upright pole standing in the middle of the floor. At their lower, outer ends they are buried in the circle of excavated soil so they shall not spread-eagle with the weight of the turf they have to carry. Cooking is done in a small pit outside; and the whole settlement is surrounded by a system of earth walls, more as a defence against wolves than human enemies.

Even in those very early times we notice the arrival of improved technical methods coming across from the mainland of Europe, the forerunners of a steady stream of ideas and techniques. The most important innovation during the centuries that followed was the introduction of metal for making weapons and implements in place of flint, horn and bone. First the rare and expensive bronze was brought in, and later the cheaper iron. Thus we have first the Bronze Age, and later the Iron Age.

Improved techniques bring a higher standard of living, and when iron axes and plough-shares became common the effect

MIDDLE STONE AGE

NEW STONE AGE

BRONZE AGE

IRON AGE

was soon seen in the homes of men. During these times there were marked differences between the standard of living in various parts of Britain. In remote and barren places there were hovels little better than the New Stone Age huts already described. These continued right on into historic times; and caves were inhabited even after Roman rule had given Britain large, well-ordered cities. However, on the whole there was a steady and continuous improvement.

For an illustration of a Bronze Age dwelling we have chosen one from Dartmoor in Devon (p. 9). It resembles the earlier ones in being roughly circular and partly excavated from the ground; but the outer ends of the sloping roof-poles rest on a low wall which gives better head room. This wall consists of two facings of stone enclosing a core of small stones and turf. There is a raised sleeping platform on one side of the hut, a slab of stone forms a hearth, and a hole in the floor nearby is used for cooking. This hut has been given a kind of porch by building a curved shelter wall outside the door, with a second outer door to one side.

The drawing at the bottom of page 9 represents one of the larger houses of the Iron Age. It belongs to the fertile South-east of Britain where timber was plentiful. The hearth is situated between four upright poles which support the upper ends of the sloping roof poles; while at their outer ends there are two circles of shorter poles. The inner of these circles may have been used to form stalls for cattle or separate cubicles for the human occupants. A hut of this size could house as many as thirty people, or a whole household with its beasts and stores.

II ROMAN BRITAIN

WHEN the Roman legions conquered southern Britain in A.D. 43 a slow but important change in agricultural methods was already taking place here. In the south and east of the country an improved plough had been introduced into certain districts—a plough that could turn the rich, lowland soils that had hitherto been left uncultivated, and could do so in one operation; whereas the primitive plough that had been in use for hundreds of years could only cultivate the infertile uplands, and that only by laborious cross-ploughing. The change was making better ground available at half the labour, and was naturally raising the standard of living. Unfortunately we know very little about the houses of Britain at the time of the Roman invasion, but we do know that a large export trade was being built up and that certain settlements were big enough to be called towns.

However, this slow improvement was as nothing compared with the spectacular changes that followed when this country was brought into the Roman Empire. Freed from the wastage of local wars and linked with the much more civilised countries on the Continent, prosperity increased with astonishing speed in many districts.

It was the official Roman policy to convert the various tribal capitals of Britain into well organised cities planned according to the Roman model. Within about fifty years these cities had been given well-paved streets laid out in an orderly gridiron pattern, and noble public buildings in the Roman style had been set up; and most of them were guarded by massive walls.

The private houses, too, which had previously been mostly round, wattled huts, were now rebuilt with squared rooms, tiled roofs, paved floors and smart colour-washed walls. Some were the simple houses of humble craftsmen, often consisting of a single long room, the street end doubtless serving as a workshop, while the tradesman's family occupied the inner portion. At the other extreme there were sumptuous establishments, with many elegant rooms ranged round colannaded courtyards.

Straight, hard roads soon linked these cities with each other and with the sea ports, whence the products of Britain could be shipped away in exchange for luxury goods from the more civilised Gaul, and even from Italy, where Rome was then the unrivalled hub of the universe.

It is true that in many country districts round, wattled huts still clustered on the hill-tops, and life there was scarcely affected by the coming of the Romans. But in more favoured

ROMAN VILLA

FURNACE HYPOCAUST

A.D. CCLXXV

PLAN

parts the local British landowners were eager to take on the Roman way of life and to rebuild their dwellings on lines similar to the elegant town houses of those days. These Romanised country houses are called " villas," a word meaning much the same as " manor house " did in later times. The nearest parallel today would be the rich " estancias "— ranch houses—of South America, with their outbuildings for ranch servants and stores.

These villas of Roman Britain are not all of one type. Some were just large, oblong buildings divided into nave and side aisles, like a church, by two rows of stout wooden pillars. In some of these there are inner walls that partition-off smaller rooms. These look like later additions, which suggests that these barn-like buildings were the earliest type of villa. In fact they may have been the type of house built by the British chieftains before the Romans came.

A more common and probably later kind is known as the corridor villa—and in which a covered corridor flanked the main range of rooms and so made it possible to pass from one to another under cover. There might be such a corridor down both sides of the row of principal rooms, or it might be along one side only. Sometimes these rooms, with their corridor, turned forwards at the ends and even at times continued right forward and across to enclose a square courtyard. This arrangement must have looked rather like the cloisters of a monastery.

On p. 12 there is a drawing of a typical corridor villa as we imagine it would have looked. The appearance of the upper portion can only be conjectured from the floors and the base of the walls, which are all that remain in position, and from the fallen debris of the upper part. Few, if any, of the houses of Roman Britain were of more than one storey. They would have looked like rambling bungalows. The one in our drawing has a corridor running right across the front of the main block, and this is balanced on the far side by a row of small rooms. These small rooms and the balancing corridor were probably lower than the block of larger rooms in between, which would have obtained light from windows placed above lean-to roofs on either side.

The walls of the villas consisted in many cases of a timber framework, filled in with wattle and daub, a mixture of clay and straw (daub) plastered onto a foundation of hazel wands, plaited like a hurdle (wattle). This type of wall had been used for centuries in prehistoric huts, and has been used in this country for humble buildings until quite recent times. Bricks, too, were used in Britain during Roman times and so also was stone; but whatever the building material the walls were usually tinted with gay colours. Roofs were covered with tiles or stone slates, and windows were filled with glass.

The more important rooms in the houses of this period often had floors elaborately decorated with patterns and pictures formed of small cubes of different coloured tile and stone, like a mosaic (p. 12). These tessellated pavements are all that survive of the decoration; but is seems certain that many of these rooms must have been gaily coloured, for fragments of brightly tinted plaster have been found.

Comfort, too, was considered, as well as appearance, for those rooms most used by the master and his family in cold weather were given a form of central heating (p. 12). A furnace (hypocaust) nearby provided the heat which passed under the floor and up through flues in the walls, thus heating the whole room evenly in a thoroughly scientific way.

The same method was used for heating those specialised forms of Turkish bath that were indispensible to the Roman way of life. The cities had their sumptuous public baths and bathing was a social activity, so the town houses seldom had baths. But no country villa would have been complete without its suite of bathrooms—cold, tepid and hot—with a deep tank for a plunge.

This brief account of the houses of Roman Britain will have been enough to show how comfortable and how advanced those dwellings were. They were not the homes of foreign officials from distant Rome, but of native Britons whose ancestors had been, perhaps, minor chieftains. The round huts of those ancestors of, say, 200 B.C. would have suggested native settlements in Basutoland or the Sudan; but a villa of A.D. 200 would not have looked entirely out of place in England today—foreign perhaps, but certainly not primitive.

EDWARD OSMOND

One bay = one rod = 16 feet

ANGLO-SAXON HALL

7th Century

III THE DARK AGES

WHILE the Roman Empire was vigorous and powerful all went well with Britain; but this country was the furthest outpost of that Empire in the north-west; and when, in the fourth century, the power of Rome began to wane, the barbarians beyond the frontiers grew daring. Then this island was soon in trouble. Repeatedly the garrison was weakened to meet pressing needs elsewhere, and each time the barbarians broke in to burn and pillage. At that time most of the villas went up in smoke; and the cities, already impoverished, were by now half ruined.

In A.D. 411 the last Roman troops finally sailed away and the Britons were left to organise their own defences as best they could. Scots from Ireland were a constant threat in the west, and the Saxons from the shores of the Baltic had for a long time been raiding the east and south coasts; but the greatest menace lay in the Picts of Scotland. A leader of the Britons tried to solve his problems by inviting a band of Saxons to come as allies and stand guard against the Picts. In that the move was successful; but the cure proved to be as bad as the disease, for the Saxons had no intention of going away again, but brought over more and more of their kindred. What had begun as a controlled movement of warriors became a great immigration—an invasion.

The Saxons were reinforced by two other nations of the same race—the Angles and the Jutes. In some districts these Teutonic immigrants found empty country where they set up their farmsteads peaceably. In other places the Britons moved westwards before the tide of invaders, or, if defeated in battle, became the slaves of the newcomers. At one time the Britons, under strong leaders, seemed to have regained the upper hand; but the tide turned against them once more, and by about A.D. 700 the whole country east of Exmoor and the Welsh mountains was firmly in the hands of the invaders.

The Teutonic settlers knew next to nothing of Roman civilisation. In their distant homeland they had known no

Early Saxon Hut (reconstruction)

settlement larger than a village, no buildings other than of timber. In Britain they gazed in wonder at the walled cities and the ruins of the painted villas, but they had no use for them. Their feelings were expressed in the words of one of their songs—

> *Cities can be seen from afar, the cunning work of giants,*
> *the wondrous fortifications in stone which are on the earth.*

So they usually gave the older settlements a wide berth, and set up their own rude homesteads in uninhabited places.

The early years of this Saxon period are very obscure, and are well named the Dark Ages. We know very little about the first Teutonic communities—how they were organised, or housed. It seems that in some places groups of free men shared the land of their village as equals, and each family lived in its own hut. On the other hand the great halls of their kings and chieftains are often mentioned in the epic songs that were handed down from very early times. In these halls the whole community seems to have shared the same roof, living a truly communal life. From this we can only suppose that customs varied from place to place, and so also did houses.

These people well understood the cutting and joining of timber. They were skilled ship-builders, and their idea of a house was very much like a ship turned upside down. They shaped the wood with an adze, which is like a large axe but mounted on its haft across-wise, like a hoe. This implement was used throughout the middle ages and, in places, until recent times. The use of stone and brick was unknown to them. Indeed bricks were not to be made again in this country for a thousand years, nor glass for about as long.

A good impression of a small house of the early Saxon period can be gained from the photograph on page 18. This shows a conjectural model of the hut of a weaver of the seventh century. Like the early prehistoric huts the floor is some three feet below ground level; and the sloping roof poles are held in position at the bottom by the bank of earth thrown up; while at the top they are lashed to the horizontal ridge-pole which is supported by two upright posts. The turf covering of the roof rests on a surface of wattle work. The ground plan of this hut is oblong but with rounded ends; thus it is half way between the prehistoric round huts and the true rectangular buildings of the more advanced civilisations.

The use of the ridge-pole allows a building to be enlarged to any required extent, a thing that is impossible in a circular building. But the longer a house of this kind becomes, the more easily can it be blown down by a strong wind if caught broad-side on. To overcome this weakness several pairs of the sloping roof-poles—called, by builders, rafters—were made extra strong to act as buttresses. And there came a time—we do not know where and when it was—when some one had a brainwave and let these pairs of very strong rafters do the work of supporting the ridge-pole. This meant that the upright supports could be dispensed with, thus leaving the centre of the floor clear of obstructions. These pairs of arched timbers leaning together came to be called crucks and they then became the main supporting members of the building's framework. Timber buildings were constructed in this way right down to the seventeenth century, and many of them can still be seen today.

The drawing on page 16 shows the hall of a chieftain built with these crucks. The framework is of sturdy oak timbers, the floor of trodden earth, while the roof is covered with turf. The upright walls between the timber framework are filled in with the same wattle and daub that we met with in the Roman villas. The main framework of such a house would probably have been set up experimentally where the trees were felled, and, if found to be satisfactory, the separate pieces would have been carefully numbered and dragged to the place chosen for the hall to be erected. There the great crucks would have been raised with the help of ox teams, and the other timbers fitted into position. In early times one spoke not of building but of *rearing* a house.

In this hall the lower ends of rafters are carried on a horizontal wall-plate, supported on upright wall-posts outside the feet of the crucks. With the floor now no longer below ground level, this is necessary to give head-room at the sides of the building. The crucks are not held in at their base by being buried in the earth, so a strong tie-beam is provided just above head level to prevent their spread-eagling, thus producing the form like a great letter A that can be seen in the drawing, and particularly clearly in the very simple stable building in the foreground.

Down each side of the hall, beyond the feet of the crucks there is a lean-to extension called an *outshot*, like the side-aisle of a church. In this outshot the cattle were stalled in some of the humbler halls; but, where the owner could afford to have separate buildings as byres, stables, granaries and so on, the outshots could be curtained or partitioned off as bed spaces for privileged persons. But the servants, and in the very early days the whole household, just lay down in the rushes that covered the floor, and slept where they could.

The square space between two pairs of crucks is called a bay. If a house has only two pairs of crucks, one at each gable end, it is a house of one bay. The hall in our picture, having four pairs of crucks, is one of three bays. These square bays measured roughly sixteen feet each way, this being the ancient measurement of a rod, pole or perch, which remained the standard measurement for a bay for hundreds of years.

A hall of this period must have been very dark, as well as being extremely dirty and uncomfortable. The hearth was in the middle of the floor, and the smoke filled the roof-space above the tie-beams, blackening the timbers with soot before it filtered out from a hole in the roof. This smoke-hole let in a little light, as well as a good deal of rain, which fell in sooty drips onto the inmates. The low door was usually left open to allow the fire to draw.

In the drawing a feast is in progress. The master of the house sits in the high seat, abreast of the fire, with his guests and relatives and servants ranged to right and left, further from the fire, in order of decreasing importance. Behind the high seat is a rich wall-hanging surmounted by the round shields of the warriors. A minstrel entertains the company, playing on the harp and chanting one of the long narrative songs of heroes and deeds of daring.

Many halls were surrounded, within their protecting ditch and stockade, by smaller buildings, as we have already seen. Among these would be one called a *bur*. This word is related to the French *beurre* (butter), and orginally meant a dairy, the place where the women's work was done. But it came to mean the women's hall, where the ladies of the household lived and looked after the young children, away from the roughness and drunkenness of the men's life in the hall itself. It later became *bower*, as we know it today.

During the six centuries of the Saxon period many changes took place. The various warring kingdoms became united, and the three peoples who originally colonised the land, having absorbed the remnants of the native Britons, had become one nation.

Anglo-Saxon England was a land of villages; but in the course of time small towns were sprinkled thinly across the face of the country. Many of these towns were fortified to act as strongholds against the ravaging Danish armies that harried the land during the ninth century; and this encouraged many more people to seek shelter within their earth and timber walls. We know from written records that overcrowding resulted. It seems clear that this led to the development of a type of house somewhat different from those in the country places, being sometimes two storeys and occasionally, at least, partly of stone. However, we know very little about these early town houses, because their remains lie deep under the foundations of existing buildings.

At the end of the Saxon period we find a pattern of society in which the villagers in many places were subject to a lord called a *thane*. He lived in a hall, surrounded by a group of other buildings—a *bur* for his womenfolk, a kitchen, a chapel with a bell-tower and a dove-cote, as well as the usual cart-house, stable, cattle-byre and granary. These would be surrounded by a ditch and stockade; while grouped outside this would be the hovels of the peasants. The thane owed loyalty and support in war to the king in exchange for the possession of his lands; while he, in his turn, exacted loyalty and service from the villagers in exchange for their share of those lands and his protection in time of trouble. This arrangement was to become crystallised during the next two centuries into a highly organised form of society, in which every member had his rights and his duties according to his position. We know it as the *feudal system*.

A late Saxon Village (tenth century)

IV THE FEUDAL PERIOD

WHEN William the Conqueror seized England in A.D. 1066, the Country contained a number of Stone Churches, but nearly all the houses were still of timber. William parcelled out the land among his own loyal supporters; and, while he set about building several great castles himself, he also encouraged the Norman lords to build smaller castles on their own estates. However, we must not think of these first private castles as great stone structures like the Tower of London. At first they would have been just normal timber halls, but with rather more ambitious earth and timber defences than had been used by the Saxon thanes. For several centuries from this time there is not a clear dividing line between a large house and a castle.

By 1066 most of the villages that we know to-day were already in existence. Each of these villages was, in fact, a large farm—an estate, called by the Normans, a *Manor*. And each of these manors was held from the king by a lord. In many cases a powerful nobleman held a number of manors, which were each managed by a steward, while the lord, with his household, led a more or less migratory life, visiting each in turn. The peasants were bound to remain on the manor in which they were born, working their own share of the land, and also working on the lord's much larger share at certain seasons.

These peasants were housed much as their forefathers had been in Saxon times. Their small huts were covered with turf or thatch. Windows and chimneys were unknown. The fire burnt on the earth floor, and the smoke lingered among the sooty roof-poles before it found its way out at the top; while in wet weather black rain dripped from the leaking thatch. Poultry and plough-oxen shared the same roof with their owners—even, in some cases, the same room—and life was hard and squalid.

The manor houses themselves must have been atrociously uncomfortable by our standards. " Safety First " was the motto in the early middle-ages, and comfort came a very poor second. However, during the twelfth and thirteenth centuries there was a steady improvement in the building of these manor houses; and, while security still received first consideration, they gradually became more generous and comfortable.

By degrees many manor houses were rebuilt in stone. Sometimes a perfectly serviceable timber hall was retained as the principal room, while the lord's private wing was re-built in a more modern form in stone. At other times the whole house, including the hall, was re-built in stone. Some of these houses still exist, though usually much altered.

We might easily be misled into thinking that all medieval buildings were of stone, because all those to be seen to-day are built of that material. The fact is that the timber houses probably outnumbered the stone ones, but naturally only those in the more durable material have survived. We know very little about the timber houses of this period, and can only suppose that they were very like those of Saxon times.

A timber hall with a thatched roof was so likely to be set on fire that it probably always stood alone. But one built of stone, its roof covered with lead or stone slates, might safely be built quite close to other buildings. So it now became customary for hall, bower and chapel to share the same roof. Farm buildings and workrooms, too, were often brought together and ranged, with the hall itself, round a courtyard for greater safety. Next to the hall were the buttery or wine store—from the French word *bouteille* (bottle)—and the pantry —again from the French, *pain* (bread)—being the food store. The names of many rooms were changed to a French form at this time, for French was the language of the ruling families. Chapel is a French word, and the English *bower* became the French *chamber*. These were usually in the same block with the hall; but the kitchen was often away by itself—an old tradition that died slowly—probably because of its incurable habit of catching on fire; for, with the smoke and sparks from the great fires rising into the roof-space, this was naturally a constant danger. But the kitchen, with the other out-buildings—stables, brew-house, dove-house and the rest—came closer together round the courtyard, often being timber lean-to erections ranged against strong stone surrounding walls.

ANGLO-NORMAN HOUSE. LATE 12ᵗʰ CEN.

FIRE PLACE ⌐
CHAPEL

BOWER

UPPER FLOOR

FIRE PLACE ⌐
HALL

BUTTERY

GROUND FLOOR

COURT YARD

STAIRS

At the same time the hall, chamber and chapel were brought together to form a kind of miniature castle keep, with the larger windows overlooking the courtyard for the sake of safety. For the same reason the hall was now sometimes placed on the upper floor, the ground floor being given over to store-rooms or stables (*below*).

The placing of living-rooms one above another confronted the early builders with a difficult problem. If the upper room was floored with timber the fire could not safely be burnt in the centre of the floor as in single-storied buildings; and in any case the smoke of the fire burning in the lower room had no means of escape. Of course if a hall was built over stone-vaulted store-rooms the problem did not arise, as it could have a hearth on its stone floor without any danger. Where a timber floor was employed the solution to the problem was, of course, to build the fireplace against the wall with a hollow chimney to lead the smoke away.

This innovation had been introduced in the manor house illustrated on page 25. Here the hall on the ground floor,

A Norman Hall (c. 1180) at Boothby Pagnell, Lincolnshire

and the chapel above it, both have such fireplaces. The bower is next to the chapel above the buttery and has no fireplace. In very cold weather charcoal may have been burnt here in a portable brazier.

The most primitive form of chimney was a hollow buttress with slits at the top on either side. The lean-to kitchen in the foreground of the picture has such a chimney; while the hall and chapel share a more advanced type, in which the buttress is greatly enlarged and a hollow stone shaft continues upwards above it.

In spite of its modern fireplaces the hall in our picture still has a bare earth floor—a custom that was to continue right on to the sixteenth century. Nor is there any glass in the windows. These could be closed in cold weather with wooden shutters. Apart from the coloured glass in certain churches, there was practically none in the country in the twelfth century. The bower and chapel are reached by an outside stairway. The chapel in a manor house of this period had many uses other than religious services, for house-space was expensive and never adequate. It served as estate office and library, for private interviews and even as a guest room if the need arose.

The hall was the focal point in the life of the manor. In it the whole household took its meals, high and low together; and here, too, was held the manor court, in which local affairs were settled and rough justice meeted out. In the same hall many of the retainers still slept—here, or in various lofts among the out-buildings—but the lord and his family had their own apartment which came to be called the *solar*, a solar floor being any floor on timber joists.

By the twelfth century the high seat in the hall had come to be placed in the middle of the end wall furthest from the doors. This further end was now the upper end, away from the draughts and the coming and going when meals were served. The servants sat at long trestle tables ranged against the side walls, the seats nearest the doors being for the humblest of those present; while the lord's family and their honoured guests sat with him at the high table. This stood on a low platform, called a *dais*, across the upper end of the hall.

Manor House

Chapel

Solar

Storerooms

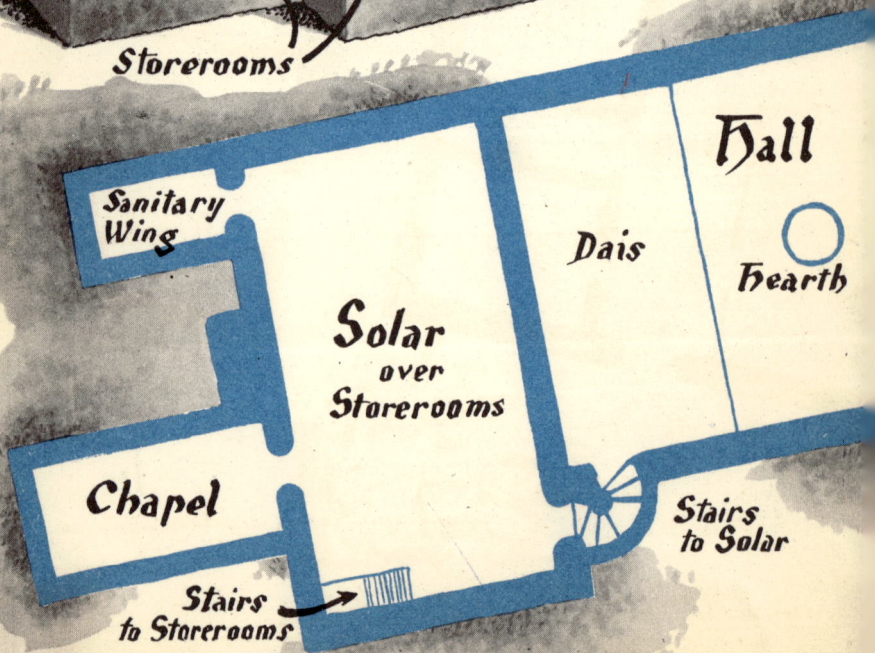

Sanitary Wing

Hall

Dais

Hearth

Solar over Storerooms

Chapel

Stairs to Solar

Stairs to Storerooms

A.D. 1250

Kitchen

Pantry

Buttery

Screens

Pantry

Kitchen

The drawing on page 29 shows an arrangement of the main rooms of a manor house that became fairly standardised during the thirteenth century. Leading off the dais at the upper end of the hall is a small doorway from which a spiral stairway winds up to the solar, which has a fireplace and is the best-furnished room in the house. There may even be glass in its windows, imported into England at great cost.

Adjoining the solar is a small chapel, and also a sanitary wing, a modern refinement that was becoming fairly common in large houses of the thirteenth century. Below the solar and chapel are store-rooms, reached, in this case, by a narrow stairway from the solar itself, so that the valuable stores could be constantly under the watchful eye of the owner, or his lady.

At the lower end of the hall two short screens, called speers, protect the long tables somewhat from the draught from the doors, while another screen in the centre leaves two openings for serving meals; and together they partition off an entrance passage that came to be known as *the screens*. From this passage two doors lead into the pantry and buttery respectively, while a third gives access to a passage leading down between them to the distant kitchen, which is still, you will note, a separate building. Above the buttery and pantry on a solar floor is another upper room, which may be used as a guest-room or for the more favoured servants.

Such a manor house with all its out buildings might be surrounded by a moat, which would also enclose the ricks, wood-pile, dung heap, and all the implements and litter of a farm yard. Poultry and doves would wander in and out of the hall, as well as my lord's hounds, while his precious hawks would occupy an honourable perch in the solar itself.

Beyond the moat would be the village of little hovels with its small stone church, and the wide fields that were shared out afresh each year among the various households of the village. There would also be common meadows for pasturing, and for hay in its season, and the waste ground beyond, all going to make up the simple agricultural unit, the medieval manor.

A Medieval Hall: Stokesay, Shropshire (c.1240) ☞

A **Manor House**

Kitchen Court

Great Chamber

Chamber

Musicians Gallery

Screen

Hall

Dais

Winter Parlour

Bay Window

Court of Honour

Porch

Dining Parlour

Late **15th century**

EDWARD OSMOND

V THE WOOL TRADE PERIOD

THE simple order of society which had developed during the Anglo-Saxon period continued under the Norman kings and on to the thirteenth century. Each village was practically self-sufficient, producing what it needed and having nothing left over to sell and therefore nothing with which to buy.

The change came very gradually at first. By degrees the villagers found that they had a small surplus to exchange for little luxuries—for things produced by specialist craftsmen in the distant town. The towns in their turn began to grow in size, with more and more craftsmen and tradesmen living within the walls. And these middle-class people, who had hitherto been so few that they were a class of no importance, were destined to become, within the next three hundred years, the most important group of people in the land. It was the stealthy beginning of one of those great social upheavals that will turn a nation head-over-heels from time to time; and the result of such an upheaval is nowhere more clearly seen than in the houses of the people.

This change was already beginning when a great calamity befell the land. An epidemic—the Black Death—swept through the squalid, insanitary houses of England, and within two years about half the population had died. The disorganisation that resulted threw the country into chaos—everywhere fields were without ploughmen, manors without lords. Houses stood empty and good plough-land returned to wilderness; and the feudal system, which had already been strained, broke down.

With English society thus thrown into the melting pot, Europe was crying out for English wool. And, with so few labourers available and land returning to waste, what was more natural than that cornland should be turned over to sheep? Thus a great national export trade in wool developed.

In a remarkably short time the people recovered from the misery and confusion that followed the Black Death, and found themselves riding on the crest of a trade boom. Peasant and nobleman alike took to keeping sheep and grew rich, while the tradesmen prospered as never before; the wool-merchants, especially, made great fortunes. The balance of society was still more upset during the fifteenth century by the Wars of the Roses, in which the nobility virtually committed suicide as a class, although certain noblemen grew very rich by raising sheep for wool. But power slowly passed into the hands of the merchants and tradesmen, and the independent yeomen farmers who had newly risen from the peasantry. From such people came the country squires of the sixteenth century. But the other side of the picture must not be forgotten; many honest peasants, driven from their land by the sheep, fell into the deepest poverty and misery.

In the two and a half centuries between 1300 and 1550 great changes are seen in houses. Existing kinds become much more modern, and new types appear. The manor houses were often enlarged by the addition of extra rooms to give greater comfort and privacy, and to accommodate larger numbers of retainers and guests. The yeomen farmers built themselves sturdy farm houses with several rooms, in place of the one or two-roomed hovels of their peasant forefathers; while the merchants in the towns now needed good middle-class houses. Yet there were many people still living in squalid shacks so primitive that we know nothing like them here to-day.

The drawing on page 32 shows a manor house of the end of the fifteenth century. The lofty hall still dominates the plan, but the master and his family no longer take their every-day meals there along with the servants as in earlier days. There is now a dining parlour on one side of the screens where the family take their meals with their guests. The kitchen and other service rooms that used to occupy this position are now ranged round the kitchen court at the back of the building, while in front is the entrance courtyard or court of honour as it was called.

Beyond the upper end of the hall the solar has become a bedroom, called the great chamber; while below it is a private sitting room known as the winter parlour. And at the other end of the hall there is a second bedroom above the dining parlour. Thus the main apartments are arranged like a letter H with the hall across the centre occupying the whole height of the building, and rooms on two storeys placed at right angles to it at either end. In some of the largest houses these two wings were extended by adding rooms called lodgings, coming right forward and across the fourth side of the court of honour, which one entered through an arched gatehouse. It was always the ambition of a wealthy and important man to be able to entertain the king and his whole retinue, for entertaining and the paying of visits were much in vogue.

These houses were still rambling, haphazard affairs; but in the main block a certain feeling of symmetry is obtained by balancing the porch which projects at the lower end of the hall by a great bay window at the dais end. The porch and the bay window are frequently the most lavishly decorated features on the outside of the building Oriel windows, too, were now in the fashion, projecting outwards from the upper storey like an ear from a person's head—hence the name, from French " oreille " (ear). There is one of these over the front door in our picture.

When we compare this house with earlier ones we notice some striking improvements. Quite a number of tall chimneys stand up among the various gables, proclaiming to the world the comforts within and the wealth of the owner. Windows, too, are now numerous and much larger than in past times, for glass is being made in England once more; and the gloomy, shuttered rooms of, say, two centuries earlier are now only for the very poor. In the bay window coats of arms blaze in the heraldic splendour of stained glass, announcing the importance of the owner's family and its powerful connections. Walls are hung with Arras cloth or pictured tapestries, and floors are often covered with patterned tiles.

The floor of the hall, however, is still strewn with rushes over the bare earth, for this tradition died very slowly. A famous Dutchman, Erasmus, visiting England early in the sixteenth century, told of the rushes being " so renewed that the substratum may be unmolested for twenty years, with an ancient collection of beer, grease, fragments, bones, spittle and everything that is nasty." So, if additional rooms were

Yeoman's House (c. 1500) at Bignor, Sussex

sumptuous with stained glass and tapestry hangings, other things had not improved at all.

Leaving, now, the lord of the manor in the luxury of his winter parlour, we must turn to the yeoman farmer, and see how he is housed in his new-found prosperity. In the fifteenth century there was no precedent for a modest, middle-class house so, when the farmer could afford something more substantial than the hut of his forefathers, he naturally turned to the manor house to provide him with a model. He adopted the H. plan with the lofty hall in the centre, and two rooms, one above the other, at either end. At one end was the parlour with a bedroom above it, and a second bedroom at the other end was built over the pantry and dairy (*above*). These houses retained the traditional central hearth, but in those that have survived chimneys have been added later.

This has happened in the house on this page which dates from the reign of Henry VIII. Notice the skilful way in which the builders have bridged over the gap at the sides left by the narrow hall: by the use of curved brackets they have con-

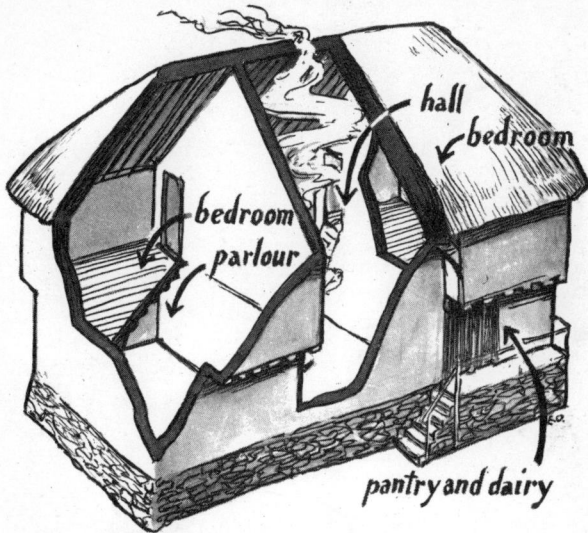

Lay-Out of the House at Bigor

trived to cover the awkward H-shaped building with a single compact roof. Notice, too the projecting upper floor which juts out abode the ground floor. This projection is called a *jetty* and it was a constant feature of two-storied timber buildings of the middle-ages.

The main reason for this jetty is a purely practical one. Floor boards rest on joists which are like very thick planks, oblong in section. To-day these joists are placed with their ends resting on the walls, and their deepest measurement upright. This gives a steady, rigid floor. But in the Middle Ages the joists were laid flat (p. 36,) with their deepest measurement across the wall, which meant that the floors tended to sag and bounce when movement took place on them. To overcome this the joists were placed to extend a little way beyond the point of support, and the upper wall, resting on this jettied portion acted as a counterbalance to hold the floor rigid. These jetties also served to protect the ground-floor walls— often of wattle and daub—from the weather; and in the towns, where the jetties overhung the narrow streets, they enabled

quite large houses to be erected on small sites.

With the increase of trade the town population was steadily growing; and the change-over from arable farming to sheep raising was causing great hardships to many people, while bringing fortunes to others. With one shepherd sufficient for a tract of land formerly served by a dozen plough-men, families were forced to leave their native villages, and many of these people drifted to the already overcrowded towns. Until the end of the fourteenth century town houses had been of two storeys only, with their narrow gable-ends overlooking the street. These houses were gradually replaced by larger ones; but, as each site was strictly limited, the only way to increase their size was to build them higher. During the fifteenth century three storeys were common; and as time went on veritable timber sky-scrapers were erected, their jettied upper storeys almost roofing-in the narrow streets (*above*).

The dissolution of the monasteries by Henry VIII, and the breaking of the ties between the church in England and in Rome, came as a great set-back to church building, but it brought fresh opportunities for the erection of large houses. The lands and wealth of the great abbeys passed into the hands of private people who were eager to display their new-found wealth by building homes to suit their status. The palaces that King Henry built have all disappeared; but Hampton Court Palace, that Cardinal Wolsey built and presented to the king, still remains as an example of a great house of that time.

There has never been a style of design more delightful or more thoroughly English than that of the houses of this reign (p. 39). Roof-lines were broken by pointed gables and many tall chimneys; windows were subdivided by mullions and transoms into many openings, each of which was surmounted by a small arch; while the whole window was capped by a squared drip-moulding to shed the rain. Inside, the fashion had turned away from tapestries as wall decorations, and instead wooden wainscoting in delightful linenfold panelling was now seen everywhere; and over the low rooms the unplastered timbers, supporting the floor above, were decorated with carvings; while the lofty halls were magnificent with great arching beams.

We should note, before leaving this early Tudor period, that bricks are with us again. Hampton Court Palace and many smaller houses were built with them. It was the Englishman's sheep that unwittingly re-introduced him to bricks, after their absence for the thousand-odd years since Roman times; for the ships that sailed from East Anglia with wool needed ballast for the return journey from the Low Countries, and what could be more suitable than the Flemish bricks? This development first took place during the fourteenth century, and by the end of the fifteenth century bricks were being made once more in the eastern counties; and from there the technique spread slowly westwards.

Wool Merchants House: Grevel House, Chipping Campden, Gloucestershire

VI EARLY RENAISSANCE

WITH Henry VIII money, like wives, did not last very long, in fact both he and his rich friends were so extravagant in their building projects that they were soon overspent, and the building of large houses practically ceased during the middle of the sixteenth century. However, the wiser policy of Elizabeth I gradually restored confidence; and during the last quarter of the century this country saw a great building boom. And now the houses built were planned on altogether different lines.

The middle-ages were over and gone, and with them Gothic architecture with its pointed arches and deep buttresses. England was no longer a backward neighbour of the great Continental nations, but was taking her place among the more advanced countries of Europe. And that Europe was bursting with new-found ideas and techniques. It was a time of adventurous launching out; and, just as men were sailing their carracks and galleons across new oceans, so they were adventuring equally in science and the creative arts—painting, poetry, music and architecture.

To make clear the changes that took place in British houses during the sixteenth and seventeenth centuries, it is well to give a quick glance back and away—away from Britain to sunny Italy, and back to the last days of the Roman Empire.

When the Angles, Jutes and Saxons slowly occupied the out-post Roman province of Britain, and in doing so obliterated the provincial civilisation that had developed there, this was no isolated incident, but a minor event similar to others that were taking place all over the Roman world. The Roman Empire, rotten at its centre, slowly crumpled up during the years that followed 400 A.D. and the barbarians beyond its frontiers streamed in to seize the spoils. Goths, Vandals, Lombards, Huns and others roved up and down those civilised lands and, like the Saxons in distant Britain, destroyed many of the wonders that they so much admired; though on the Continent the destruction was less thorough than in Britain.

16th CENTURY

ROME **A.D. 100**

FLANDERS **ITALY**

ENGLAND
A.D. 1590

EDWARD OXFORD

But although the military power of Rome was gone, she slowly reconquered the heathen barbarians by means of her Christian missionaries, and in time gained spiritual control of Western Europe, including Britain, through the Popes.

In matters of art and science, also, Rome was not dead, but only dozing, while her sister city in the East, Byzantium, was very much awake. Those relics of Roman artistry that remained in sculpture, writings and architecture always exerted some civilising influence on the Church-ruled world, as it slowly emerged from the barbarism of the Dark Ages. And, in time to come, when the authority of the Church began to weaken, men were free to dip more and more into the age-old storehouse of ideas and forms that still remained of the work of Roman writers and artists; and those ideas and forms were born again, with all the vigour and joy of youth, in that great movement of minds that we call the Renaissance.

The focal point of this movement was naturally Italy, that storehouse of things Roman. Rome, Venice, Florence, Padua and scores of other cities began to blossom with buildings whose forms, Roman in origin, were now used with a new freedom. By degrees this Renaissance architecture was taken as a pattern by builders further afield; but in France it was mixed with native French forms and produced a mixed style. Further away still in the Netherlands and Germany, where, even in ancient times, Roman influence scarcely penetrated, it was naturally modified still more, and was mainly seen in Roman details looking strangely ill-at-ease on buildings of purely northern form. Thus it came about, in the sixteenth century, that Renaissance ideas first reached England from these lands where Renaissance design was least understood; and it was only later that Englishmen were able to study pure Renaissance work in Italy. So, in this country, the new style arrived, as it were, in instalments; and the first attempts to achieve it were sometimes very strange, though often delightful.

During the reign of Elizabeth I many foreign craftsmen came to England, most of them Catholic refugees from the Low Countries. Moreover Englishmen who had been abroad, on trading missions, perhaps, or with the army across the North Sea, had seen and admired the new Renaissance buildings,

The Great Chamber (1585) *at Gilling Castle, Yorkshire* ▶

13th Century

STAIRWAYS

Stone Spiral

Oak

Mahogany

Iron

Stone

Elizabethan

Pine

Restoration

Regency

and the foreigners found ready employment here for their skill.

The settled state of the country, and this influence from overseas, finally convinced the English squire that he need no longer live in a miniature castle, with all its larger windows overlooking an untidy courtyard. So the new houses turned their gaze outwards, and great windows full of abundant glass could at last safely give views of the distant landscape. A house was now considered as a whole and designed to look imposing from a distance. Like those on the Continent it had to be balanced exactly, on either side of the main entrance. The rooms were made more lofty and the whole building raised to be three, or even four, storeys high. Several steps led up to the front door to give dignity, and terraces often raised the house above the gardens to add to the effect of height and to give a wider prospect from indoors. How different from the haphazard castle-like houses of only a century earlier.

The drawing on page 41 shows a typical manor house of this period. Notice the balustraded terrace with steps leading down to the trim garden below, and the doorway with its round Roman arch and flanking columns on their square pedestals. these are arranged in exactly the same way as they would have been in the days of Roman rule thirteen hundred years earlier. Notice too the great bay windows rising up two storeys high and the oriel window over the doorway. The curves and angles of the many gables are an adaptation of the Flemish style, but typical of Elizabethan design; and equally typical are the groups of tall chimneys and the balustrades along the eaves.

Those who planned these houses did not always find it easy to keep them strictly symmetrical, as the new fashion required. The builders of the Middle Ages had made no attempt at exact symmetry when erecting a house, so it never distressed anyone then that the main doorway should be right away at one end of the hall. Now, however, the main doorway must be dead central in the whole facade, and yet most English squires were set on retaining the traditional arrangement of hall, with an upper and lower end.

Obviously something had to be sacrificed, and it was usually

Montacute House, Somerset (1580-1601)

the size of the hall that was reduced. With a smaller hall on one side balanced, beyond the sceens passage, by a parlour much larger than usual, both ancient usage and modern fashion were reconciled.

The hall of an Elizabethan house sometimes occupies the height of two storeys; but, with the other rooms so much taller than they were in the older houses, this was not only unnecessary, it made the hall inconveniently lofty. So it was usually no taller than the other rooms on that floor.

A remarkable feature of the houses of this time was a great, elongated room called the *long gallery*. This was often many times as long as it was wide, and frequently occupied the whole length of the top floor of one of these tall houses. One of these galleries was nearly always included in any large house of Elizabeth's reign and the thirty years that followed; and they are typical of this period only. These long galleries tell us much of the increased wealth of the country gentlemen of that time, for they had no utilitarian purpose, but were simply used for pleasure and ostentation. To give up the greater part of one floor of one's house to such non-essential purposes would have been unthinkable a century earlier.

The change to the Renaissance style affected the decoration of the inside of houses also. Fireplaces were often surrounded by carvings—coats of arms, strap-work patterns, Roman columns, pilasters, nude figures in pseudo-Italian style, and many other devices were brought together in arrangements that were often more ornate and robust than they were tasteful. The same applied to the hall screen that was often equally lavishly carved, with gilding and colour added.

But, if carved decoration was not invariably tasteful, plaster work was nearly always delightful. The art of the plasterer was new in this country, having been brought in by refugees from abroad; but it immediately found a place in the Elizabethan home. The decorated plaster ceilings of the time, though a complete novelty then, are perhaps the most beautiful and also the most thoroughly Elizabethan feature of the large houses of those days (p. 43).

What a luxury these new ceilings must have seemed! The unceiled floorboards of previous years had allowed both

664) Ye LLANDOGER TROW.

draught and noise to pass through unhindered to the upper rooms. Now the continuous surface of plaster made the upper room much warmer and also gave much greater privacy.

But it is time to leave the comfortable mansions of the squires and wealthy merchants, and find out how the humbler folk are faring. We have seen how, in King Henry's time and earlier, the wool trade had brought great poverty as well as great riches. The plight of the poor people, thus deprived of a decent livelihood, became so bad that in Elizabeth's time statesmen had to take steps to improve the lot of these paupers, who were living either as squatters in flimsy hovels along the roadsides, or in the cities where old mansions had become squalid tenement houses and newer buildings had been raised storey upon storey to meet the pressing need for house-room. The homes of the poorest people in the country were so flimsy and so primitive that they have long since been abandoned and disappeared without trace or record. But a few farm-houses remain from this time, mostly having a lofty hall in the middle, where the fire burned in the centre of the floor, and rooms on two storeys at either end. These have usually been altered since by giving the hall a chimney so that a floor could be added above it, thus providing a continuous upper storey across the whole of the house to give an extra bedroom above the hall. This was to become the usual pattern for cottages and farm-houses in future years.

Burford Priory, Oxfordshire (c. 1640)

VII LATE RENAISSANCE

WE must now pass on to the time of Charles I, for the next big change in British houses. This occured when a certain young man returned from Italy, full of enthusiasm for the wonderful Renaissance buildings that he had seen there, and especially those designed by the great Italian architect, Andrea Palladio. This young man's name was Inigo Jones, and he became one of our greatest architects. King Charles commissioned him to design a great banqueting hall for an enormous palace that he intended to build at Westminster. This great hall gave its name to Whitehall in London, where it can still be visited today. It was the first building in England to be erected in the true Renaissance style. Jones also designed a house for the Queen at Greenwich; and he or his pupils were responsible for a number of large country houses designed in the manner of Palladio, whose style was so distinctive that it gave a new adjective to the English language; we still speak of it as " Palladian."

Poor Inigo Jones was born at an unlucky time. His patron, King Charles, was soon at war with Parliament—a quarrel that sent him to his execution—and many of the richer people, who had supported him, were forced to fly for their lives across the sea. No time, this, for costly building projects! Small houses were replaced, of course, when necessary; but very few large undertakings were put in hand.

However, bad times pass; and in 1660 Prince Charles returned, with much rejoicing, to receive his father's kingdom. Then, too, the exiled royalists could return to their homes and estates.

These people had seen many new things during their travels abroad—churches, palaces, mansions—many of them designed in the most up-to-date Styles. And, once home, they wanted houses that were equally up-to-date. It was not now the case of just a few rich people fancying Palladian houses; the whole country was ready and eager for the new style, and many people really began to understand it.

This understanding of Renaissance design was increased by the growing popularity of foreign travel, particularly during the eighteenth century. Then any young man who claimed to be of " the quality " considered it necessary to go on the " grand tour"; to see for himself all the glories of France, Italy and Ancient Rome. Books, too, were published on architecture, and many English gentlemen became competent amateur architects; professional architects, also, went abroad to study the new style, for the designing of buildings had now become a separate profession. In earlier centuries the man who planned a house, in so far as it was planned, was just the most experienced and gifted workman employed on the job; but by degrees the designing and the erecting of a house came to be done by different people, and the demand for a unified design finally brought about a complete specialisation.

From the time of the Restoration of Charles II to the throne, for about 170 years, the story of British houses tells mainly of a constant attempt to reach a compromise between the ideals of Palladio and other recent architects in Italy, and the deep-seated traditions of the average Englishman—that is to say, between the ideas of Ancient Rome, new-born after more than a thousand years, and those of the barbarian Anglo-Saxons, refined and educated somewhat but not altered. Differences of climate, too, necessitated a further compromise, for a style invented to contend with the excessive light and the heat of a Mediterranean country was unsuited, in many ways, to the cold and gloom of this northern land.

There were certain people, it is true, who so much admired the Italian buildings that they attempted no compromise, but chose to live in houses that were Italian in every way—even close copies of existing houses in Italy. Some of these buildings are very fine and impressive, but they look cold and out-of-place in this country, with their white marble columns and wide expanses of unbroken wall-surface. Rooms lined and floored in various coloured marbles may seem deliciously cool on an August afternoon in Italy; but they are almost unbearable early on a February morning in England. In exaggerated example of these Italianate mansions white marble goddesses

FIREPLACES 14th Century

Elizabethan

Late Georgian

The Moot House, Downton (c. 1650)

recline dangerously above the elaborate doorways, and carved cupids romp round the friezes, while all the inhabitants of Mount Olympus flounder about on clouds on the ornate painted ceilings.

These extreme examples of the Italian taste, however, are very rare. In most cases an excellent compromise was arrived at. The details of style changed somewhat—the periods are known as *Restoration*, *Queen Anne*, *Early* and *Late Georgian* and *Regency* (early nineteenth century)—but most of the changes were slight and only a few of the main ones are important enough to mention here.

Let us look first of all at the Italian ideas and ideals. Italian design at its best was very grand and noble, with a great sense of style; at its worst it tended to be too sensational and grandiose. The Italian climate needs small windows and

A Restoration Staircase: Tythrop House, Oxfordshire (c.1680)

EARLY GEORGIAN

A.D.1730

ROMA

EDWARD
OSMOND

wide surfaces of wall, giving cool, shady interiors, a low-pitched roof is permitted, for snow is not a menace, columned loggias and porticos are an advantage and little or no provision is made for heating. Moreover, Italy has plenty of good building stone, including beautiful marbles, but not much large timber. Many of these conditions are, of course, reversed in Britain; and British architects struggled manfully to retain the best in Italian design while fulfilling the requirements of another climate and nation.

If we compare the house illustrated on p. 55 with the earlier one on p. 32, we see clearly the adjustments that have been made. Notice the exact balance to right and left of the dignified entrance, the strong horizontal line of the cornice under the eaves, the low-pitched roof and unobtrusive chimneys. These are all concessions to the Italian taste, and yet this house is altogether English. Where the topmost rooms would have been lit earlier by windows set in the tall gables, they now have dormer windows placed on the slope of the roof, which is hipped, that is to say it slopes back from all four sides. The only kind of gable that is fashionable now is the low Roman pediment. The height of doors, windows, and even of the ceilings is now controlled, not just by the height of the people living in the house as it was in earlier times, but largely by the need for dignity and good proportion in the whole design. People sometimes preferred to put up with great inconvenience in order to achieve a suitable effect.

A hundred years earlier the roof-line of a house would have been broken by a forest of chimneys (p. 41), gables, finials (upstanding ornaments) and weather vanes. Now the silhouette must be as simple as possible. Sometimes the chimneys, and even the whole roof, would be concealed by a balustrade, for even the humble farmhouses now have one or more chimneys which are no longer rare enough to be boasted about—moreover they were un-Italian.

The front elevation of a house, if not all its aspects, was now planned to give the most imposing effect. Windows must balance exactly. If a big window was needed on one side of the central doorway to give light to a large living-room, the corresponding one on the opposite side must be

Blenheim Palace, Oxfordshire (1705), *designed by Sir John Vanbrugh*

exactly the same size, even though it lit a tiny pantry.

This anxiety about the outward effect of a house was not entirely due to the needs of the Renaissance style; it also sprang from the mental attitude of the average person of this period. After the great social upheavals of the sixteenth century and the strife and uncertainty of the civil war, society settled down for a while to a comparatively static condition. People became rather rigidly partitioned off into fixed classes; and each family had to accept its position, high or low, in society and make the best of it. The squire, the parson, the shopkeeper, the groom, the labourer were taught that " God made them high and lowly, and ordered their estate," and on the whole they accepted this situation gratefully enough. But each household was naturally anxious to maintain its allotted position in society and, if possible, to better it. So appearances counted a good deal, and the seemly appearance of the residence came second to none.

For the richer people servants were plentiful, and the largest houses needed an army of them. Often there was a basement or semi-basement (p. 56), in which this army worked and fed, while it slept in poky attics in the roof. Sandwiched between these secret, unvisited regions were the principal apartments in which the favoured few lived and entertained their guests, for the paying of long visits was a favourite pastime of the leisure classes.

The appearance of the inside of the house was considered nearly as important as the outside. The lofty rooms were as splendidly furnished and decorated as the owner could afford to make them. In the greater mansions the tall windows looked out on to parklands in which the whole landscape had often been re-designed to give a noble and attractive view. Whole villages were removed to achieve this, and lakes and small Roman temples were set in their place. Of course such great parks and mansions were only for a few, but they were the ideal and envy of all and sundry.

In these great houses the walls were covered at first with mural paintings or tapestries, while in the simpler taste they were panelled. This panelling was enriched here and there with festoons of carved decoration executed most

An Adam Room (c. 1773): at 20 St. Jamess Square, London 🖝

An Adam-Style House at Mountsorrel, Leicestershire

skilfully in wood. Introduced into these festoons were flowers and fruit, birds and animals, armour, cannons, and all manner of objects, as the fancy of the householder suggested. Stair-rails, too, were often richly carved, for the staircase of a large house had slowly emerged from the narrow spiral stairways of the medieval days, and now took a proud place in the centre of the house (p. 54). Richly modelled plaster ceilings continued to be popular, and so did oil paintings, at first framed into the panelling and later becoming portable as we know them.

During this time trade with the Far East was opening up; and the great East Indiamen were rolling home with samples of porcelain, lacquer work, carpets and many other things from distant places. In their cargoes they brought wallpapers

Georgian Symmetry at Barnfield Crescent, Exeter (1798-1800) ☞

from China which immediately became popular; and this inexpensive form of wall covering was soon being produced here, no doubt to the great relief of the middle-class householder who was struggling to keep up appearances befitting his station in life.

Another innovation was the sash window (p. 55). The new style necessitated simple openings, unbroken by the many stone mullions and transoms of earlier years. There is a limit to the size to which a hinged casement can be made, so the very large undivided windows popular in this country could be opened and closed only by sliding them up and down, with a concealed lead counter-balance suspended on a sash cord. Hinged casements were now only used in humble houses and in small dormer windows and the like.

Over the greater part of England red brick was now the most common building material. The forests had largely been felled in previous centuries so timber was less plentiful, and building with flint or stone was difficult and tedious; so now that bricks were cheap and abundant, and being much more durable than wattle and daub, they were adopted everywhere, and a uniformity of style resulted. Now for the first time good cottages for the humblest workers could be built, and the shacks and hovels of earlier times were mostly abandoned.

The second half of the eighteenth century saw a distinct change of style, though it only affected the details of designs. Just as Inigo Jones, more than a century earlier, had studied Palladian design in Italy and returned to practice it here; so now the brothers Adam made a study of Ancient Roman work, returning home to begin a revival of that style. One of these brothers especially, Robert Adam, had such a strong influence on the fashion of the time that this late Georgian period is often called the Adam period. He had spent some time helping to excavate the ruins of a great Roman palace, built by the Emperor Diocletian in A.D. 300 at Spalato on the shores of the Adriatic. In doing so here, and in Italy, he had gained a great knowledge of Roman design, and was so impressed with it that he resolved to work in the same style himself.

Late Georgian
c. 1790

Drawing Room   Hall   Eating Room

Brunswick Square, Hove (1825), *designed by George Busby*

On p. 61 there is a photograph of a room designed by Robert
Adam on his return home, in which you can see the care with
which he carried out this idea down to the last detail. Statues
in the Roman manner were very popular, and rooms were
sometimes furnished with niches ready to receive them. Walls,
tinted in soft colours over the smooth plaster, were adorned
here and there with very dainty plaster decorations. The same
delicate plaster work was seen on ceiling. In fact, at this times
all interior decoration tended to become dainty and refined.

This clean, precise kind of design was continued, with a
slight difference, during the early part of the nineteenth
century—often called the Regency period. Tall pilasters and
slender Roman columns were very popular. Outside walls
were given a smooth surface of stucco; and slate was used for
roofing, even in London and other towns, far from its place of
origin. Cast iron, too, was coming to the fore, and balconies
with canopies were popular in the towns, while cast-iron
verandas were often added to country houses.

Pelham Crescent, London, designed by George Basevi (1820-30)

Early Victorian

Rooms
at back
of House
↓

Maids'
Room →

Spare
Bedroom
→

2nd
Drawing
room →

Morning-
room →

Scullery
↓

Hall.

E.O.

Town Houses c1840

Rooms
at front
of House
↓

3rd FLOOR
— *Nursery*

2nd FLOOR
— *Best
Bedroom*

1st FLOOR
— *Drawingroom*

GROUND FLOOR
— *Diningroom*

BASEMENT
— *Kitchen*

PLAN of
1st FLOOR

DOWN
UP
UP

STREET FRONT

*Steps
to Area
and
Tradesmen's
Entrance*

A Regency Gothic Villa at Cheltenham

During the Regency period the influence of Roman thought in architecture was brought to its logical conclusion in this country in the form of town planning on a small scale. The great ideal that underlay all Ancient Roman thought was that of *order*, a quality very foreign to the northern mnid. During the Middle Ages it was in the abbeys only that this ideal had been given visible form, and on their dissolution it had begun to find expression in private houses. We have seen order and balance slowly develop during nearly two and a half centuries, and now we find groups of houses arranged to form a single design (pp. 66, 67).

Much of the charm of our towns and villages up to this time had lain, and still does lie, in the contrast between one house and its neighbour. Now in certain places a different effect, equally delightful in its way, was obtained by arranging entire streets, or crescents or squares, in carefully ordered designs.

A Regency Classical Villa at Cheltenham

MID-VICTORIAN

A.D.   186.

EDWARD OSMOND

VIII THE INDUSTRIAL PERIOD

THE reign of Queen Victoria saw another great social upheaval, after the long period of comparative standstill. Its cause was nothing so tranquil as the sheep that had led to a similar upheaval three hundred years earlier. This time it was machines, factories, mass-production—the Industrial Revolution in fact. This was already having an effect on the materials of which buildings were made—an effect that has continued to our own time—but now it caused great changes among the people who lived in those buildings and commissioned their design. It was one of those periods when society seems to come to the boil, and certain families burst up to the top and others are sucked under—a process that is, of course, always going on, but is accelerated at such times.

Now the industrialist was coming into his own; and, what is more, he was " coming into money"; and the old, ordered society was ending. Factories were drawing thousands of people into the fast-growing industrial towns. Most of these were poor people, leaving country occupations to become factory hands. Vast areas of slums were built to take them. There the small houses in straight rows stood face to face and back to back, their front doors opening directly on to the pavements, their back doors into a tiny yard, divided by a low wall or fence from the equally tiny yard of a house in the next street (p. 72).

A discreet distance away, the employers had their own elegant homes. They wanted houses that possessed a gentility worthy of the social position of the owners, whose own gentility was often only recently come by. In fact many of these new-rich knew very little *about* gentility; but they secretly compared themselves with others whose forefathers had, for centuries, trained themselves in social refinement, and, for that reason, they were the more anxious about the appearance of their houses. The results were sometimes very ridiculous.

REVIVALS

British architects, through their devotion to Palladian, and then to Roman forms, had no longer any native, British way in which to build. For some time they had been experimenting with ideas borrowed from the Middle Ages (Gothic) or from Morocco or elsewhere. These experiments continued. Pseudo-Greek, Pseudo-Tudor, Pseudo-Gothic houses were designed. They were built in yellow brick or grey brick or brick of a harsh glaring red, so different from the soft, rosy bricks of earlier days. The Gothic style, particularly, was revived on a large scale, both in large buildings, like the Houses of Parliament, and in quite modest houses—even in farm cottages. The results were sometimes good, but often very bad. Gables, balconies, dormer windows, turrets and all the apparatus of past years were often combined without rhyme or reason (p. 72). A new invention, the conservatory, was nearly always added on; and the mass-produced plate glass gave the windows a blank appearance that was very foreign to the Gothic style in its own days.

Splendid attempts were made here and there to restore a sound common-sense into building, and some very lovely houses resulted; but public taste had become so corrupt that these examples, being few, had practically no effect, and the lesson has not been properly learned even today.

During Regency and Victorian times town houses were becoming more or less standardised. The aim was to achieve large houses on very narrow sites, so they were sandwiched together in long rows, each individual house being a narrow tower of rooms, usually two to every storey (p. 68). The kitchen and scullery were in the basement, where the tradesmen's entrance was reached through a pit-like area. On the lower floors the sitting-rooms were placed, while above that the bedrooms and nurseries rose in pairs, with the maids' bedrooms surmounting the lot in the attics under the roof. Through the whole height of the house rose the stairway, zig-zagging up through four or more storeys from the basement to the attics.

Just inside the front door of such a house was a small square space, which boasted the time-honoured name, *hall*. Believe

The Italianate Revival in Holland Park, London (c. 1845) ☞

it or not, this little space was the direct descendant of the great timber halls in which the Anglo-Saxon chieftains quaffed their mead and munched their venison. From being the whole house, it became first the banqueting-hall, then the noble vestibule, and finally shrank to become the small space at the foot of the stairs. But we must respect this little hall, for all the other rooms of the house are really just additional amenities added on to it.

We must not leave the Victorian period without mention of the great blocks of flats which then became a feature of town life. Here individual dwellings were arranged one above another, each on a single floor. During the last hundred years flats have been built for all income groups—for the poorest people in the form of tenement houses, and upwards through all grades to the luxurious service flats of the very rich.

Since the days of Queen Victoria there has been a great deal of experimenting in house construction, and also in design. On the whole houses have become simpler and more sensible. We have seen the red brick and smart, white-painted woodwork of the early years of this century; and the very simple steel and concrete houses of the years between the wars, looking like so many cardboard boxes placed together. We have seen council houses, usually admirably simple and serviceable, and occasionally real architectural masterpieces. We have even seen aluminium *prefabs* delivered by road, ready-made. Besides these and others which have been free from the fault of imitating past styles, there are still houses being built that aim to gain character and effect by apeing the past without understanding.

What the future has in store we shall learn in time—" He that pays the piper calls the tune"; and in the new buildings to be erected in our own time, we shall get only what we ask for. Let us ask for something sane and simple and gracious; something worthy to stand beside the many lovely houses that we have inherited from past centuries.

Four centuries of Porches: (top left) at Sheldons, Wiltshire (fourteenth century): (top right) at Kirby Hall, Northamptonshire (c. 1570); (bottom left) at Sutton Courtenay, Berkshire (c. 1720); (bottom right) in Dublin (c. 1780)

INDEX

The numerals in **heavy** type denote the page numbers of the illustrations.